W9-BCI-668

811
MYE   Myers, Walter Dean,
                1937-
C. 86
              Brown angels.

                              34880030037886

$15.60

DATE			

Brown Angels

WALTER DEAN MYERS

Brown Angels

AN ALBUM OF PICTURES AND VERSE

HarperCollins*Publishers*

ALSO BY WALTER DEAN MYERS

Scorpions

The Mouse Rap

Now Is Your Time!
The African-American Struggle for Freedom

The Righteous Revenge
of Artemis Bonner

Photographs on pages 8 and 16 used by permission of
the Library of Congress. Photographs on pages 12, 22, 31, 37 (girl on
bicycle and baby in basin), and 39 used by courtesy of the Richard Samuel
Roberts Estate. Photograph on page 25 used by permission of the Oregon
Historical Society. Remaining photographs are
from the author's collection.

Brown Angels
An Album of Pictures and Verse
Copyright © 1993 by Walter Dean Myers
Manufactured in China. All rights reserved.

Library of Congress Cataloging-in-Publication Data
Myers, Walter Dean, date
  Brown angels : an album of pictures and verse / by Walter Dean
Myers.
      p.   cm.
  Summary: A collection of poems, accompanied by photographs, about
African American children living around the turn of the century.
  ISBN 0-06-022917-9. — ISBN 0-06-022918-7 (lib. bdg.)
ISBN 0-06-443455-9 (pbk.)
  1. Afro-Americans—Juvenile poetry.   2. Children's poetry, American.
[1. Afro-Americans—Poetry.   2. American poetry.]   I. Title.
PS3563.Y48R45   1993   92-36792
811'.54—dc20   CIP
                                                                  AC

❖
First Harper Trophy edition, 1996

Brown Angels

Blossoms

I never dreamt
that tender blossoms
would be brown
Or precious angels
could come down
to live in the garden
of my giving heart
But here you are
brown angel

Love That Boy

Love that boy,
like a rabbit loves to run
I said I love that boy
like a rabbit loves to run
Love to call him in the morning
love to call him
"Hey there, son!"

He walk like his grandpa
grins like his uncle Ben
I said he walk like his grandpa
and grins like his uncle Ben
Grins when he happy
when he sad he grins again

E. A. Moore,   Crystal Springs,
Photographer.   Miss.

His mama like to hold him
like to feed him cherry pie
I said his mama like to hold him
feed him that cherry pie
She can have him now
I'll get him by and by

He got long roads to walk down,
before the setting sun
I said he got a long, long road
to walk down,
before the setting sun
He'll be a long stride walker
and a good man before he done

Zudie O, Zudie O

Zudie O, Zudie O
Chug on down
Swing your hips
All round the town
Zudie O, Zudie O
What you see?
Fine black boys
From Sangaree
Zudie O, Zudie O
Where you been?
Akuba-Lan
And back again
Zudie O, Zudie O
Where you going?
Anywhere
The Wind is blowing

Prayer

Shout my name to the angels

Sing my song to the skies

Anoint my ears with wisdom

Let beauty fill my eyes

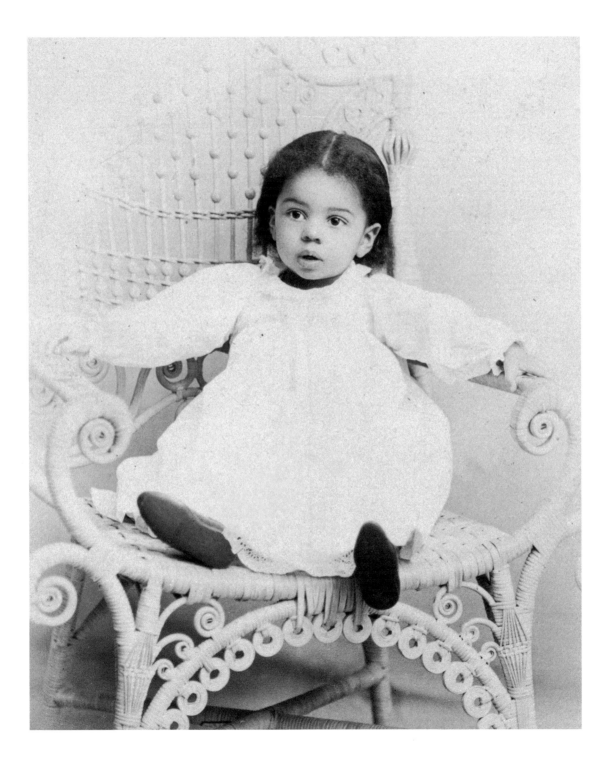

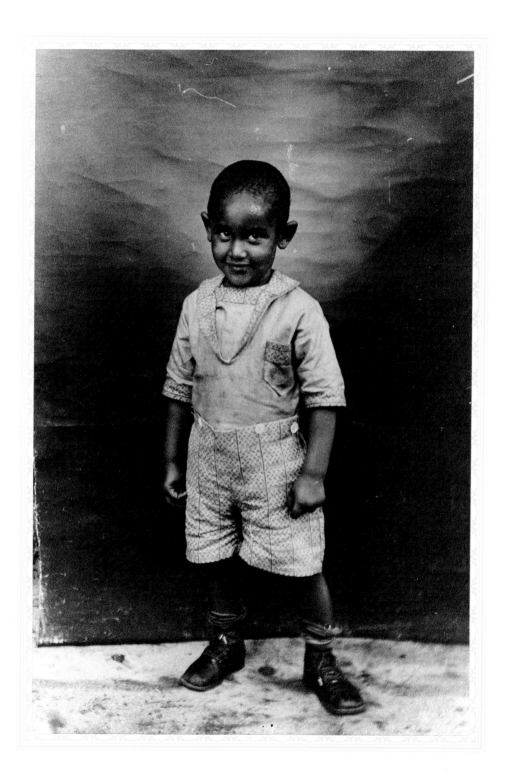

They

They say you don't know a blessed thing
Ain't that something?
Say you just smiling cause
You don't have nothing else to do
You ever hear of such a thing?

I think it's them old folks

Who don't know nothing

Them with their old serious selves

A-scuffling and a-snuffling

And being so tizzy-busy

They don't remember

How good a grin feels

Ain't that something

How people forget that?

Ain't you surprised?

I thought you would be!

Jolly, Jolly

Jolly, Jolly, sweet and brown

Jolly, Jolly, gee

Jolly is the lucky child

Who looks like me!

Summer

I like hot days, hot days
Sweat is what you got days
Bugs buzzin from cousin to cousin
Juices dripping
Running and ripping
Catch the one you love days

Birds peeping
Old men sleeping
Lazy days, daisies lay
Beaming and dreaming
Of hot days, hot days,
Sweat is what you got days

Pretty Little Black Girl

Pretty little black girl
Sweet as you can be
Wiggle waggle, wiggle waggle
One, two, three

Pretty little tan girl

She knows all the tricks

Wiggle waggle, wiggle waggle

Four, five, six

Pretty little brown girl
You know you sing so fine
Wiggle waggle, wiggle waggle
Seven, eight, nine

Pretty little coffee girl

She knows how to win

Wiggle waggle, wiggle waggle

We've reached ten!

Jeannie Had a Giggle

Jeannie had a giggle just beneath her toes
She gave a little wiggle and up her leg it rose

She tried to grab the giggle as it shimmied past her knees
But it slid right past her fingers with a "'scuse me if you please"

It slipped around her middle, it made her jump and shout
Jeannie wanted that giggle in, that giggle wanted out!

Jeannie closed her mouth, but then she heard a funny sound
As out that silly giggle flew and jumped down to the ground

Jeannie caught it with her foot just beneath her toes
She gave a little wiggle and up her leg it rose

Pride

The sound of their steps

has long been gone

Black foot, strong foot,

stumbling on

Oh follow the memory!

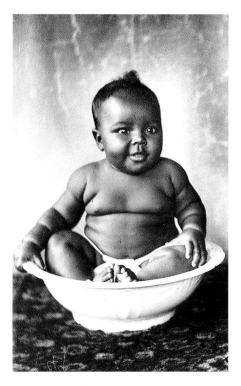

The sound of their song
has long been gone
Black song, strong song,
souls singing on
Oh cherish the memory!

The depth of their pride
will never be gone
Black hearts, strong hearts,
hearts beating on
Oh honor the memory!